Did God Really Say
THAT?

Also by Steve R. Bierly

Help for the Small-Church Pastor

How to Thrive as a Small-Church Pastor

My Own Grief Observed: Christian Essays on Aging, Suffering, Death, and Grieving

Stronger Than Spinach: The Secret Appeal Of the Famous Studios Popeye Cartoons

Sex and the Single Guy: What the Bible REALLY Says

Watching Movies with God and My Friends: A Small Group Discussion Guide

Why I Won't Let Go Of God: A Personal Defense of My Christian Faith and The Basics of the Christian Faith

Wrestling with God: The Normal Christian Life

Did God Really Say THAT?

12 Tips on How to Read, Understand, and Apply the Bible

by
Steve R. Bierly

Copyright 2017 by Steve R. Bierly. All Rights Reserved

Appendix 3 was originally printed in *Sunday School Guide*. It is used by permission.

All scripture quotations, unless otherwise indicated, are taken from the Holy Bible, New International Version®, NIV®. Copyright ©1973, 1978, 1984, 2011 by Biblica, Inc.™ Used by permission of Zondervan. All rights reserved worldwide. www.zondervan.com The "NIV" and "New International Version" are trademarks registered in the United States Patent and Trademark Office by Biblica, Inc.™

Design by Deborah Bierly
Printed by CreateSpace, an Amazon.com Company
Available on Kindle

Dedicated to my wife, Deborah, my daughter, Abigail, and all the Bible teachers I have had down through the years.

NOTE:

The stories in this book are true, or are composites of real situations, unless otherwise stated.

Table of Contents

Introduction: God Said It, I Believed It, And Now I'm All Mixed Up! 9

Tip 1: Remember What The Bible Actually Is 17

Tip 2: Realize That The Bible Is Not Primarily God's Personal Message To You 23

Tip 3: Let The Authors Of The Bible Debate, Clarify, Enlighten, Contradict, And Correct One Another 33

Tip 4: Follow The Progression Of Themes And Ideas Within The Bible 45

Tip 5: Recognize Jesus As God's Ultimate Revelation To Humankind 57

Tip 6: Don't Sweat The Stuff You Can't Understand 65

Tip 7: Let The Church Guide Your Interpretation Of Scripture 71

Tip 8: Give The Biblical Authors The Right To Talk Like Real People Do 77

Tip 9: Remember That God Is The Hero Of The Bible 85

Tip 10: Realize That The Bible Is A Call To Action...93

Tip 11: Feel Free To Skip Some Parts......................101

Tip 12: Don't Study The Bible As A Purely Intellectual Exercise 107

Appendix 1: For Further Study...............................113

Appendix 2: Six Common Mistakes People Make When Approaching Bible Study 117

Appendix 3: An Exercise in Misapplying the Bible 121

Appendix 4: Thirteen-Week Study Guide 127

One Last Note From The Author 157

Introduction: God Said It, I Believed It, And Now I'm All Mixed Up!

When people read the Bible, strange things can happen - things that are not at all what the original authors of the Bible intended. Consider the following examples:

- Christians living in Nazi Germany supported Adolf Hitler and his atrocities because they believed the Bible taught that the government authorities were ordained by God and that Christians should respect and obey them (see, for example, Romans 13:1-7).
- A strange loner on a Christian college campus uttered prophecies against the students and The Christian Church by claiming Ecclesiastes 3:1 as his authority for doing so,

declaring that, since the Bible said there was a time and a season for everything, it was now his time and his season.

- A woman maintained both that the Bible teaches that true believers won't suffer the hardships of aging (Psalm 1:3; 92:12-15; Isaiah 40:28-31) and also that her godly husband needed to give up his construction business because he was getting too old and having too many aches and pains to continue doing that sort of work, and yet she sensed no incongruity in her beliefs.

- Young people give up on the Christian faith because they read the "fairy tales" the Bible is supposedly full of, and the commands for genocide God gives (see, for example, Joshua 9:24-25; 1 Samuel 15:1-3), and the passages that suppress women, treating them as inferiors (see, for example, Ephesians 5:22-24; 1 Timothy 2:11-15; 1 Peter 3:1-7).

- Christians believe the United States

must support the state of Israel in everything it does, right or wrong, even if atrocities are committed against Palestinians, because the Jews are "God's chosen people" (see, for example, Genesis 12:1-3; 31:24; Zechariah 2).

• Believers struggle over whether or not they are actually Christians because they don't speak in tongues, and therefore must not have received the Holy Spirit when they supposedly made a commitment to Christ (Mark 16:17-18; Acts 2:1-21; Acts 10:44-48).

• Sincere Christians follow Jesus but can't understand why their prayers for healing, prosperity, solved problems, and improved circumstances are never answered, especially since the Bible promises believers these things (see, for example, Exodus 23:25-26; Deuteronomy 11:13-15; 28:1-14; Psalm 103:1-5; Matthew 6:25-33; 21:21-22; John 14:12-14; James 5:13-18).

Let's face it! Interpreting the Bible is hard work. And it gets confusing and frustrating at times. Why else did you pick up this book except that you have been frustrated and confused yourself at times. And we've all made mistakes in interpreting and applying the Bible.

Some mistakes Christians make when it comes to the Bible are pretty harmless. For example, a child reads "Blessed are those who are persecuted because of righteousness, for theirs is the kingdom of heaven" and focuses on the "persecuted" part, taking it to mean that God notices and cares when bullies pick on him at school. Although this is not the full meaning of the passage, it still fits in with the bigger picture of what the Bible teaches. No harm, no foul.

But other mistakes can be devastating to individuals and even to nations and to The Church Of Jesus Christ. Consider these examples:

- We read in our history books of kings who sent armies to retake Jerusalem from the infidels because the Bible supposedly claims that it is God's Holy City and is supremely important to him and to his plans.
- Churches deny women the use of spiritual gifts that God gave them because the Bible supposedly teaches that women can't lead congregations.
- From firmly held, yet mistaken beliefs, cults and heresies spring up.
- Christians live lives of quiet desperation, believing, because of the way they understand and interpret Bible passages, that either God is letting them down or that they are letting God down.
- Parents beat up, or psychologically and emotionally abuse their children because the Bible says that children are full of foolishness but the rod will drive it from them.
- Preachers and teachers tell half-truths

or even total falsehoods about God.

- Christians have a shallow, superficial understanding of scripture, so that when the deep waters of trouble or challenges or doubts or temptations pour over them, they are easily uprooted and swept away.

- Groups of Christians push their own particular versions of "The Truth" and belittle, dismiss, and even downright hate anyone who disagrees with them.

Every Christian and every Christian group interprets the Bible and decides how to apply it, or not to apply it, today - even those Christians and groups who claim to "accept the Bible exactly as it is." For example, not many Christians today greet church members of their same sex, or even the opposite sex, by giving kisses even though the Bible commands us to do so (1 Corinthians 16:20; Romans 16:16, 2 Corinthians 13:12; 1 Thessalonians 5:26). We say that this command doesn't apply to us, and we substitute hand shaking instead. But we have made a judgment call in order to do so. If we see a pretty married person and lust after him or her, we don't then gouge out our eyes and throw them away as Jesus commands us to do (Matthew 5:27-30), because we have determined that his words aren't to be taken literally. We don't stone people living among us who follow the ways of other religions or execute believers who turn from The Way (Deuteronomy 17:1-7). We say that the commandment no longer applies in our day and age.

We all make judgment calls concerning how to interpret, understand, and apply the Bible. And because we all do it, let's make sure we're doing it correctly.

This book is meant to help us hear and understand what the Bible is really saying. It's not meant to be the last word on the subject or to be a comprehensive and complex textbook. It's written for real people like you and me, not professors. So,

I'll give 12 tips that, hopefully, will keep us from messing with God's Word so that we won't end up messed up ourselves or messing up a world that desperately needs to hear messages from the Lord. And hopefully, these tips will spur your own thoughts and spiritual growth onward and add to The Church's ongoing discussion of how to read, understand, and apply the Bible.

Tip 1: Remember What The Bible Actually Is

The question was asked during a Children's Sermon, "How does God talk to us?"

A little boy piped up with an answer. "One time he came down out of the sky to tell us about Moses."

I'm not exactly sure what that boy was referring to, but some people share his view of divine revelation: God reaches down out of the sky and hands us the Bible. From heaven to us in one easy step! A direct gift from the divine realm to the Earth. Oh, humans were involved somewhat in the process, but when they were, God sort of took possession of them and made their writing hands move as though they were operating a Ouija board.

Or else God dictated his memoirs to his human scribes and they dutifully took down every word he said exactly as he said it.

But throughout the history of the Christian Church, that view of the Bible hasn't been the dominant one. It only arose fairly recently in response to what some believers feared was a liberalism that undercut the authority of the Scriptures. But for centuries, Christians looked at the Bible as being exactly what it is - God's Word in human form using human thoughts - without feeling that the Bible's authority and integrity were threatened. The Bible is a collection of sacred writings from various authors from different periods of time, even from different centuries. God inspired the authors, yes, but he used their own particular writing abilities and styles, their own personalities, their own reflections and observations and meditations, their particular concerns, their research, the ideas and literary forms they borrowed from their cultures and their neighbors around them, and their vocabularies in order to communicate his Word to us. The Bible didn't come directly from heaven to our doorsteps, but came through human "middlemen."

The Bible is God's Word incarnated, meaning that God's message comes to us via humans, through flesh and blood beings, just as Jesus is the ultimate message of God to us – God's Word made flesh (John 1:14). This poses some difficulties for us as we try to understand the scriptures.

Because human vocabulary is sometimes inadequate to talk about the things of God, and God is too big for human minds to grasp, the biblical writers sometimes struggle with their thoughts and how to express them. We will also struggle to understand the writers and to follow their thoughts.

Even Jesus, the ultimate incarnation of God's Word, was often misunderstood. The crowds didn't know what his parables meant, religious leaders wondered how the son of a carpenter from Nazareth could claim to be the great "I am," and how he could claim to be able to destroy the temple and in three days build it back up again. People didn't get what Jesus was saying. They had to work hard to understand what he meant. In the same way, we have to work hard to understand the incarnate Word of God in the Bible.

When Jesus came to earth to live as a human, he gave up some things in order to limit himself (Philippians 2:5-8; Matthew 24:36). In the same way, when God chose to use human authors from particular historical periods, he limited himself by communicating his message through their limitations. He spoke through their limited understandings of science, geography, ethics, the nature of the universe, etc.

Jesus, the incarnate Word, suffered abuse at the hands of men. Even his followers with whom he spoke clearly oftentimes didn't grasp what he was saying. Likewise, the incarnate Word that is the Bible has also suffered abuse at the hands of its enemies, and even its friends don't always grasp what it is saying. There is evidence that even the biblical writers themselves sometimes didn't comprehend what God was telling them and that they didn't fully understand what God's messages to them, and through them, were (1 Peter 1:10-12). Just as Jesus was subject to human weaknesses while he was bodily here on the Earth (Matthew 21:18-19; Luke 22:44; John 4:6-7), so God's Word coming to us through the human writers of the Bible was subject to their weaknesses. Just as Jesus, the living, literal, ultimate embodiment of God's Word to us, learned and grew over time (Luke 2:41-52; Hebrews 5:8-10), so the biblical authors incarnating God's messages also learned and grew over time. On many subjects, there are progressions of thought in the Bible which clarify, and even correct, earlier ideas. (There will be more about all of this later in the book.)

The Bible is God's written revelation to us of his character, his nature, his power, his ethics, his plans, his actions, his love for us and the world, and our place in his kingdom. But God used humans to communicate his revelation. Just as Jesus is both God and human, so the Bible is both the product of the divine mind and of human minds. It is both godly and very human. Accept the Bible as being a gift both from heaven (God) and from earth (humans from different periods of history and different cultures). If you do, and take both the heavenly and earthly aspects of the Scriptures seriously, you'll be saved from coming up with some weird interpretations and applications of biblical passages.

Tip 2: Realize That The Bible Is Not Primarily God's Personal Message To You

The story is told of a man who would close his eyes and flip through his Bible every day. Then he would randomly jab his finger down on a page, open his eyes, and begin reading wherever his finger had landed. He believed that what he found there was God's message for him on that particular day.

One day, his finger landed at, "Then he went away and hanged himself."

Shaking his head, he thought, "That can't possibly be God's message for me!" He tried again.

This time his finger landed on, "Go and do, Thou, likewise!"

Well, let's hope the man didn't "go and do

likewise," but the story makes an important point. The Bible is not a fortuneteller, or a fortune cookie, or an astrologer, giving us personalized supernatural messages each day. It's also not a self-help guru offering you daily words to live by.

The Bible is indeed God's message to you, but this is because the Bible is God's message to his people. And you are one of those people. The Bible is addressed to The Church corporately, as a body, as a whole. Since you are a member of the corporate Church and are part of the body, the whole, God's message is addressed to you. But it is not *primarily* a message addressed to you as an individual.

Think of the President giving an address to the nation on TV. Some parts of the address may really hit home for you and apply to you. But the President didn't mention your name or say, "I'm talking to you, (*insert your name*)!" Like the President giving an address, the Bible is God giving an address to his nation, the New Israel, The Church.

It becomes, in a real sense, his message to you, as the Holy Spirit takes what he says and allows it to really hit home for you and shows how it applies to you. Preachers and teachers also are God's instruments to bring the Bible home in this way.

The letter of Romans, for example, was written primarily to Christians living in Rome in the first century A.D. It wasn't written specifically for American Christians living in the twenty-first century. But throughout the centuries, the Christian Church has recognized that the letter contained many universal truths that were applicable to all God's people everywhere, so The Church made the book of Romans part of the Bible. Modern day readers will find many relevant spiritual truths for today in Romans. But modern day readers don't have to look all over their towns for Tryphena and Tryphosa in order to greet them as Paul commands (Romans 16:12).

Certain great speeches such as The

Gettysburg Address, John F. Kennedy's "Ask not what your country can do for you," and Martin Luther King Jr.'s "I have a dream," stand the test of time, not because the speeches were addressing us personally, but because they contain eternal, unchanging truths.

We should consider the Bible to be a collection of classic speeches, stories, and sayings that, while not specifically addressed to us, nonetheless stand the test of time because the concepts they present are eternal.

We must remember that the biblical writers were addressing their own particular historical situations, not ours. They dealt with the concerns of their own days, not ours. Because God is timeless and he doesn't change and human nature never really changes and "What has been will be again, what has been done will be done again; there is nothing new under the sun," many aspects of the writers' messages are applicable to us today. But not all aspects.

Here are some examples of writers addressing their own particular concerns and how their words can be misinterpreted today:

- Though people today search the books of biblical prophecy to determine what's happening in our world, the book of Revelation wasn't describing how the Anti-Christ's army will rise from Russia or the Middle East in the future. It was talking about the persecution, and relief from it, that believers living close to the Apostle John's day were experiencing, or would soon experience.

- When Jesus prophesied about people fleeing for their lives and some being left behind, and an abomination being set up in the temple (Matthew 24), he wasn't talking about a future one-world government led by the Anti-Christ, or about the rapture, or about a restored temple in the 21st century. He was referring to the fall of

Jerusalem in 70 A.D. and the horrors leading up to it and after it.

- Jesus told his listeners to "seek first the kingdom of God," but despite the way the verse has been used by some modern preachers, Jesus didn't have in mind how white middle-class males living in the United States could deal with their midlife crises and find renewed purpose, but rather how we should sacrifice all for God's kingdom and trust God to provide for all our needs.

- The Old Testament gives rules and commands for Holy War that many people today would find unenlightened, even barbaric, but these commands were given to a nomadic people who were former slaves, looking for a home in a hostile region of nations that God had already judged because of sin. The rules and commands don't deal with how we are to treat our enemies today, nor about current border disputes between Israelites and Palestinians.

- Prophecies about Jews returning to their land weren't fulfilled by the establishment of the modern state of Israel in 1948, but were instead fulfilled when the ancient Hebrews returned to Palestine after being exiled to Babylon. This was viewed as such a miracle, that religious leaders at the time referred to it as a "Second Exodus."
- When Paul and Peter wrote about men and women's roles, they were addressing how Christians could live peaceful, fruitful, productive, and witnessing lives in a world where women were uneducated and where female temple and cult prostitutes were the norm in pagan religions. The Apostles weren't even remotely considering a world like ours where women go to public and private schools and can become judges, CEOs, Prime Ministers, professors, and Presidents.

Not only was the Bible not primarily written to us, it also wasn't written in the styles that we modern readers prefer. For example, strict chronology and continuity and slavish attention to detail while reporting stories weren't important to the Gospel writers. So, for example, John puts the cleansing of the temple early in Jesus' ministry while Matthew, Mark, and Luke place it near the end of Christ's life. And Matthew has Jesus cast out demons from two possessed tomb-dwellers into a herd of pigs, while Mark only talks about one demoniac. What was important to the writers of that day was themes, not timelines or details. And some modern readers have balked over the seemingly inflated and inconsistent numbers that appear in accounts of battles and peoples in the Old Testament. But that's the way the authors wrote back in those days. They weren't concerned with exactly and precisely how many troops perished. They wanted to convey feelings and ideas and get the big pictures across. Every detail didn't have to be perfect. And what about all of those "who begat who" lists in the Old Testament and the recounting of all who returned to the land after the exile? While we would never put such boring stuff in our devotional literature today, it was important to the original readers to know who their ancestors were and what they did. Their culture placed great value on this.

Understanding the times and the mindsets and the original audiences of the biblical authors is important if we are ever going to understand and comprehend what they wrote and not be shaken by the discontinuities and discrepancies between their worlds and ours.

Tip 3: Let The Authors Of The Bible Debate, Clarify, Enlighten, Contradict, And Correct One Another

Years ago I attended a seminar about evangelism. The speaker was instructing us how to handle common objections non-believers raise to Christianity.

"If someone says that the Bible is full of contradictions, ask the person to point some out to you. He or she won't be able to do it because chances are he or she hasn't ever read the Bible and is just parroting back something heard long ago from someone else. Anyone who reads the Bible knows that it isn't full of contradictions," he asserted.

Well, I hate to contradict the speaker, but the more I've gotten into the Bible, the more I see that it's only people who HAVEN'T carefully read the Bible who believe it doesn't contain contradictions. In fact, the more I read the Bible, the more I see that it is full of contradictions!

Here are a few of them:

- Deuteronomy and Proverbs teach that if you live a righteous life, you will prosper materially and be healthy, well-liked, etc. Job and Ecclesiastes say that bad things happen to the best of people and that you can't judge a person's righteousness, or unrighteousness, by the way a person's life turns out.
- Proverbs 16:31 believes that old age is a blessing. Ecclesiastes 12 says that old age is the pits.
- Hebrews 10:3-4 tells us that it is impossible for the blood of bulls and goats to take away sins. But you certainly wouldn't get that impression from reading Leviticus and Numbers!

- 2 Kings 10 gives the Lord's approval to Jehu's slaughter of the people in Jezreel who were loyal to Ahab. But the Lord's word in Hosea 1:4-5 is that the house of Jehu will be punished for that massacre.
- 2 Samuel 24:1 says that the Lord's anger burned against Israel, so he incited David to take a census of the fighting men. Retelling the story of the same incident, 1 Chronicles 21:1 says that Satan rose up against Israel and that it was he who incited David to take the census.
- In 1 Samuel, Chapters 17, 18, 23, 27, and 30, David's prowess in battle and his rise to power are attributed to the Lord. The Lord even commands David to do battle. 2 Samuel tells of the war between the house of David and the house of Saul, and of David's conquest of Jerusalem and the Philistines, concluding that "...he became more and more powerful, because the Lord Almighty was with him." (2 Samuel 5:10). But in 1 Chronicles 22:6-10, God won't

let David build the temple because David had shed "much blood and had fought many wars." David had "shed much blood on earth" in the Lord's sight.

- Deuteronomy 12 tells the Israelites that they are to have one place of worship. The rest of the Old Testament makes it crystal clear that this is the city of Jerusalem. However, when Jesus, who was God made flesh, ministered on earth, he spent most of his time outside of Jerusalem and told the Samaritan woman that God seeks those who will worship in spirit and truth, regardless of their physical or geographical locations (John 4:19-24). And those times when Jesus went to Jerusalem, he got into trouble! He called it the city that kills prophets and stones the ones God sends to it (Matthew 23:37).

- Paul tells us that salvation is by grace through faith and not by works (Ephesians 2:8-9), and that our righteousness is based on faith and comes to us from God through Christ

(Romans 3:21-5:21). The book of James, though, seems to be saying that Christianity and salvation are all about works, works, and works!

- In Mark 10:1-12, the Pharisees tell Jesus that, according to Old Testament Law, it is okay for a man to divorce his wife. Jesus replies that Moses only wrote that because humans are so hard-hearted, but that God's best and original plan has no room for divorce.

- The book of Exodus teaches both that Pharaoh stubbornly hardened his own heart against the Lord and was responsible for the consequences (3:19; 5:2; 7:13-14; 8:15, 32; 9:34) and that the Lord was the one who hardened Pharaoh's heart so that the Lord would be glorified in the miraculous deliverance of the Israelites from Egypt (7:3-4; 9:12; 10:1-2, 20, 27; 11:9-10).

- Proverbs 26:4 warns, "Do not answer a fool according to his folly, or you will be like him yourself." The very next verse commands,

"Answer a fool according to his folly, or he will be wise in his own eyes."

And I can't even begin to list the many biblical passages that teach that God is in control of everything that happens - predestining us according to his plan - alongside the multitude of verses which teach that our destiny is up to us and that our choices really matter!

Should contradictions shake our faith in the Bible as God's inspired, authoritative Word? I must admit that as I was first discovering them, they shook my faith! And I, like many Bible-believing Christians and scholars, have attempted, and still attempt, to harmonize them and/or to find ways to explain them away. Some contradictions can indeed be explained by using the principles found in this book. But I now believe that we should let some contradictions stand as contradictions. We can even praise the Lord for them. Why?

The Bible deals with supremely complex subjects - God, eternity, morality, the meaning of life, lessons we should learn from history, spirituality, etc. When we humans deal with complex subjects, we can't help but contradict ourselves, because complex subjects can't be summarized, or even explained, neatly and cleanly. Years after the end of World War II, controversy still rages over whether or not we should have used nuclear bombs against Japan. On one hand, the war was shortened and lives were no doubt saved. On the other hand, the devastation was beyond anything the world had ever known. Since there are two or more sides to issues we humans deal with, why should we expect the ways of God to be simple and straightforward? For example, when looked at one way, the crucifixion of Jesus Christ was a travesty of justice and the ultimate act of humanity rebelling against its creator. When looked at another way, however, it was God's greatest victory. And it may have been necessary in God's wisdom for King

David to subdue his enemies with God's help, but on another level, God preferred that his king would be a man of peace.

I can hold two contradictory views at the same time, and I'm certainly not as complex as God. For example, part of me wants my kids to live with me forever, while another part of me wants them to go out in the world and make their own lives. I even know that it is necessary that they "leave the nest" and do so. But there's still the "empty nester" in me which wants them around. If I, with my small brain and small heart, can be contradictory at times, why can't God be with his massive brain and gigantic heart?

Or, suppose I want to give a young person instruction on the best way to live life. I might use two old sayings that contradict one another. "Look before you leap!" and "He who hesitates is lost!" Both are true in different circumstances and at different times, though both sound mutually exclusive.

Sometimes as I listen to representatives of different political parties debating issues on TV and contradicting each other, I realize that The Truth is probably somewhere in-between their extremes, and I'm glad I heard the opposing points of view because they led me to my own conclusions.

Also, a friend and I can be talking about a problem or a plan or an idea and the friend can bring up something that seems contradictory to my way of thinking. But it opens my eyes in new ways and I say, "I never saw it that way before!"

The Bible makes contradictory statements that are nonetheless true depending on the circumstances and times. It will also present opposing points of view so that we can synthesize them and find The Truth somewhere in the middle. God doesn't want us to see things only from one point of view, so he presents many ways of looking at things in order that we'll say, "I never saw it that way before!" And God lets authors further explain what other authors meant. He even lets authors correct wrong impressions that other authors give.

Yes, I said, "wrong impressions." Remember that God used humans to write the Bible. Humans are fallible. They misread situations and misinterpret what God is doing. This doesn't mean that mistaken passages should be excised from the Bible. God wants them in there as examples to us of how NOT to think and act. For example, the portions of the Bible that were written after the Babylonian Exile were correct in calling on the people to trust in the Lord, to hope for God to do something glorious in the future, and to renew their covenant with him. They were wrong in overemphasizing nationalism, racial purity, the importance of Jerusalem and the temple. How do we know this? The New Testament is against nationalism and racism, and renders Jerusalem and the temple irrelevant. Still, God wants us to read the post-exilic literature because we, too, have prideful tendencies which could lead us to link God's plans to our group, our race, our area, our cherished beliefs and our sacred cows. We are much like those authors and can see ourselves in them. The post-exilic literature is also a case study in what the fear of repeating the mistakes of the past can do to people in the present.

Truth is sometimes contradictory. For example, there's no easy answer to the question, "What is light?" Scientists have discovered that light is sometimes particles and sometimes waves, even though it seems to their minds as though both can't be true. And to compound the problem, the nature of light changes depending on the observer's beliefs and expectations! In the case of light, the answer is "Both/And," not "Either/Or." And in the case of so many of the aspects of God and his dealings with us, the answer is "Both/And," not

"Either/Or." We should learn to be more like the peoples of the Far East and of the Middle East and embrace contradictions, and realize that contradictions often describe the nature of reality.

When we read and study the Bible, we need to let its authors debate, clarify, enlighten, contradict, and correct each other. We shouldn't be content with just pulling verses or passages or books out here and there from the Bible. And if God wants to use Author #2 to explain to us what Author #1 meant, why should we stop after reading only what Author #1 wrote? If we don't read Author #2 as well, how will we know what God is REALLY saying to us? We need God's full revelation, given through humans, to us and not be content with just part of it. This means that we should always be moving toward knowing what the whole Bible says about its subjects.

Tip 4: Follow The Progression Of Themes And Ideas Within The Bible

    Imagine meeting someone claiming to be a true blue, rabid *Star Wars* fan who said, "I wonder who 'The Other' last hope that Yoda mentioned in *Episode Five* is. And will we ever find out if Darth Vader is really Luke Skywalker's father? Are Han and Leia doomed to be apart forever?" You might look at him strangely and ask, "Haven't you ever seen *Episode Six: Return Of The Jedi*, or any of the prequels?" What would your reaction be if he said, "No, and I don't want to. I just want to endlessly wonder about the story and be frustrated." You'd think there was something seriously wrong with this individual and would be sad that he was missing out on so much.

Have you ever been reading a book that was too good to put down? You just had to turn the page and find out what happened next, or what was really going on, or who the villain was operating behind the scenes. You wouldn't dream of placing the book up on a shelf and never looking at it again.

When Barack Obama was elected President, many articles and news features and documentaries traced the history of Black people in America from slavery to the Emancipation Proclamation to Reconstruction to Brown Versus The Board Of Education to the Civil Rights Movement to multiculturalism and so on, concluding that the United States had been moving for quite a while toward the direction of having a Black President, and that it was a question of "When" we would have one, not "If" we ever would. The day the Civil War ended we certainly weren't ready to elect a Black President, but the seeds of the idea were already there.

What do all of these things have to do with interpreting the Bible? I'm glad you asked. If we don't read the whole Bible, we will miss out on the full story of what God has done. It would be like a so-called *Star Wars* fan who never watched *Episode Six*, or like someone returning a mystery novel to the library without ever knowing how it turned out. And just as there have been political and social movements throughout American history that predicted where we would go as a country, there are progressions of thought and of ideas in the Bible which reveal to us the directions God wants his people to go, even if at the time the Bible was written its authors weren't quite ready to go all the way there yet.

Why did God reveal some things in piecemeal fashion? Why didn't God reveal all he wanted to say to people all at once? Well, how could he? He is infinite and the minds of the biblical authors were finite. He didn't want to literally blow their minds. Also, he is a compassionate Father who meets people where they are at. Some of the ideas and plans of God were too much for authors and audiences living in their cultures, with their built-in mindsets and lifestyles, to swallow all at once. So God graciously took things slowly.

Let's briefly look at just a few themes and ideas which demonstrate progression throughout the Bible and show us where the Lord wanted, and still wants, his people to go:

- The earliest way to deal with sin in the Law of Moses was to offer sacrifices to the Lord. But later, many of the prophets taught that offering sacrifices without changing the lives of the continually sinning people and the correcting of societal sins and evils was useless. The New Testament then presents Jesus and his sacrifice on the cross as the ultimate answer for our sins. Paul says the cross is our way to God and that the old way of sacrifices has been abolished

(Ephesians 2:14-20), and the author of Hebrews asserts that it was actually impossible for the Old Testament sacrifices to take away sins - instead those sacrifices had pointed toward Christ (Hebrew 10:1-10). So, the theme of offering sacrifices for sin pointed towards, and climaxed in, the crucifixion of Christ. And the crucifixion of Christ touches the hearts and lives of people in ways that animal sacrifices never could, making them willing to forsake their personal sins and work against the evils found in their world.

- How do you live a long, happy life according to the Bible? Well, the Law of Moses is pretty clear - obey all the commandments explicitly and you will live long lives blessed by God, disobey them and be miserable and die. But the books of Job and Ecclesiastes say, "Not necessarily." And biblical characters like David and Jesus and his disciples broke the letter of the Law and yet were blessed because of it (Matthew

12:1-8). The Old Testament prophets moved away from the written law by talking about God giving his people new hearts and a new spirit so that they would know the Lord and obey him. The New Testament commands us to follow the Law of Christ, which basically means that we are to love others as Christ loved us. Paul says that the written Old Testament Law couldn't prevent sin. In fact, it had the opposite effect (Romans 7:7-25). To Paul, the Old Testament Law kept humanity in slavery so that we would look to Christ to liberate us, and it was a tutor to keep spiritually immature children in line until Christ arrived on the scene (Galatians 3:15 - 4:11). Paul admonished the Colossians not to let anyone judge them by whether or not they obeyed the food and drink and Sabbath and religious festival rules found in the Old Testament (Colossians 2:16-17). And the Jewish believers in the early Church felt that the Law had been a burden to them and they didn't want to saddle Gentile

Christians with it (Acts 15:1-21). The Bible shows that the Old Testament Law was good and necessary for a time, but that it has been superseded by the better Law and by the Spirit of Christ. While I was in seminary, and then throughout my early years as a pastor, there was a group within Presbyterian circles that believed we all needed to go back and enforce The Law of Moses as the Law of our lives and of our land. Then, we would be blessed by the Lord. After all, they reasoned, God's law is perfect. Yes, but in the Bible God's revelation to us moved away from literal obedience to a written code and toward obeying and following the spirit of love behind all of those rules. And the New Testament - contrary to the Law of Moses and following the Old Testament lead of Isaiah 53 - makes martyrdom, instead of living a long, full, healthy life, one sign of being blessed by God (John 15:18-16:4, 21:19; Acts 7:54-59; 20:22-24; Hebrews 11:35-38; Revelation 6:9-11; 7:13-

17; 20:4-6).

- Though many books in the Old Testament talk about wars and holy wars, and vengeance on the enemies of God's people, and an "eye for an eye," the book of Jonah implicitly questions all of this. And Isaiah and Zechariah picture the coming Messiah as a man of peace (Isaiah 9:6; Zechariah 9:9-10). Jesus dismissed the "eye for an eye" ethic and told his followers to turn the other cheek. He said that God is good, even to his enemies (Matthew 5:38-48). Jesus even forgave those who crucified him as he hung on the cross. Later on in the New Testament, we are told to leave revenge up to the Lord. Paul wrote that the only "vengeance" appropriate for a Christian was to do good works for enemies (Romans 12:14-21), and he reminded us that we are fighting, not against people, but against spiritual forces (Ephesians 6:12). Paul gives the state the right to bear the sword, but only to punish evildoers and ensure the peace. Clearly, the movement in scripture is away from physical warfare and toward spiritual warfare, and away from violence toward love.

- While the Bible never comes right out and unequivocally grants women equal status and power with men in The Church, it certainly moves in that direction and, therefore, we can be confident we're doing God's will when we move in that direction today. In Genesis, Man and Woman are both made in the image of God and are given authority over creation (Genesis 1:26-28). In Genesis 2, when God makes Adam a "helper suitable for him," the Hebrew words used there imply that Eve is the one who redeems Adam from loneliness because she, out of all created things, can meet him face-to-face, eye-to-eye, as an equal. Despite the Bible's great introduction to Eve, the rest of the books of the Old Testament Law, including the rest of Genesis, can indeed at times make it seem as though women primarily cause trouble for men and that women, like slaves, are property. But at least the Law of Moses does treat wives, daughters, and female slaves better than the laws of the surrounding cultures did at the time. And the Bible tells the stories later of Rahab who saved the Israelite spies, of Deborah who was a judge in Israel, and of Ruth and Naomi who set the stage for their descendant, David. The Bible also lists several women who were given the title "prophetess" and the Bible recounts the story of how a king, through his religious and governmental leaders, consulted the woman Huldah to find out what God's will was. And it describes how Abigail saved David from committing a grievous sin that could have jeopardized his future, recounts how Esther saved the Jews from extermination, and includes the divinely inspired words a king's mother taught him as part of the book of Proverbs. The New Testament shows us Jesus teaching women - which was unheard of for a rabbi to do in that day. It also uses women as God's first witnesses to Christ's resurrection, even though testimony of women was considered unreliable in the courts of that time period. While it is true that Paul, (writing to people living in a patriarchal world in which women were seldom educated and in which women in the predominate pagan religions and cults served as temple prostitutes) restricted the role of women in The Church, he also said that in Christ there was no male or female; he called women his co-workers, and named one woman as an Apostle (Junias in Romans 16:7). Whew! It seems pretty clear that the Bible slowly moves women toward full liberation in Christ and complete participation in the life, and leadership, of The Church.

- There are some Christians today who await the rebuilding of the temple in Jerusalem so that sacrifices can once again be offered to God. They forget that the Bible moved from a literal interpretation of Israel, the temple, sacrifices, and Jerusalem to more spiritual ones. Israel is now The Church (Galatians 3:29; 1 Peter 2:4-10), the temple is Christ's body (John 2:19-21; 2 Corinthians 6:15-16), his death put an end to sacrifices (Hebrews 9:11-10:18), and we await a Jerusalem from heaven (Revelation 21:2-4), not the establishment of an ideal one on Earth.

If we're going to understand what God is really saying to us in the Bible, we've got to follow the progressions of its themes and ideas. Otherwise, we may be stuck in "God Episode Five" when he wants us to move on to "God Episode Six."

Tip 5: Recognize Jesus As God's Ultimate Revelation To Humankind

Have you ever heard someone say, "That's my last word on the subject?" What he or she probably meant was, "I've said all I have to say and couldn't really add anything to what I've said, or say it any better than I already have." Or, "I'm not ever going to change my mind about this."

Well, Jesus is God's "last word" to humanity. He is God's ultimate, perfect revelation to us (John 1:1-2, 14-18; Hebrews 1:1-4; 3:1-6), and his apostles, having been trained by Jesus Christ and following the same Spirit that led Christ, carried on his ministry of revelation (Matthew 16:17-19; 28:18-20; John 14:25-26; 1 Peter 1:10-12). God's not going to ever say anything better than he has said it through Christ, nor is he ever going to change his mind and go back on anything he said in Christ.

If you wanted to experience the Mona Lisa, you could look at a child's drawing of that famous painting. Maybe you could tell that it was a picture of a woman who had a strange expression on her face. Is it a smile or not? And you would know that something about the Mona Lisa intrigued the child enough so that he or she wanted to make their own copy. Maybe you would want to know what was so intriguing about the original, and you'd investigate further. Then, later, you might see a reproduction of the painting on a poster hanging on an art major's wall in a college dorm room. Ah, now you understand what's so intriguing about the Mona Lisa. But if you ever got a chance to visit the Louvre and saw the actual masterpiece, you'd say, "Wow! As much as I liked that poster, there's nothing like the real thing!"

Or suppose you want to visit the statue of a

famous general in a park. As you approach the statue, you can see parts of it through the trees and get a sense of what it looks like. Getting closer, you can see the shadow of the statue on the ground and once again get some sense of the statue itself. But finally, when you are at the statue you can see the real thing, look it up and down, walk around it, and touch it.

The Old Testament is like a child's picture of God, or an art major's poster of him. It's like God glimpsed through the trees of a park - like God's shadow cast throughout history. These things are good and intrigue us and capture our imagination and inform us about God and make us want to experience more of him. But Jesus is the real masterpiece. He is God himself that we can look at up and down, walk all around, and touch by faith.

The Old Testament sets the stage for Jesus' arrival. We wouldn't know how important he was without the background information and the set-up the Old Testament provides. We wouldn't recognize him as God if God hadn't already been introduced to us in the Old Testament. We wouldn't recognize our need for him without the Old Testament showing us what we are like and what our lives and world are like. And Jesus, the man, was Jewish and was steeped in the Old Testament's ways. In order to fully understand Jesus, we need the Old Testament. So, the Old Testament is important. But Jesus is God's supreme revelation and the fulfillment of all the Old Testament is about.

So, if you are reading the Old Testament and become puzzled about God, don't despair. Those writings are many centuries, and many cultures, removed from you. And the God in them is the God who is still shadows, the God who is still saying that no one can see his face and live. It is no wonder, then, that we puzzle over some aspects of God and his dealings with humanity as we read the Old Testament. When we find ourselves scratching our heads in confusion, we should turn to Jesus and his apostles for a clearer picture of who God is and what he desires. They give the clearest picture of God we will receive this side of eternity.

For example, though there are many parts of the Old Testament which show us that God is the God of the whole world, he does seem to focus the majority of his attention in those ancient documents and stories on the Jewish people. Is God ethnocentric and is his religion a religion almost exclusively for descendants of Abraham? Well, Jesus says that those who do the will of God are the ones who are truly his brothers, sisters, and even his mother (Mark 3:31-35). Jesus healed Gentiles and praised their faith. He said that when he was lifted up on the cross, the whole world would be drawn to him. Paul said Jesus destroyed the dividing wall between Jew and Gentile and asserted that everyone who has a faith like Abraham's is a child of Abraham. Jesus and his apostles clearly give us a

God who is for the whole world. Abraham's example of faith and the promise fulfilled through him and his descendants, and his ultimate descendant, Jesus Christ, brought blessings to everybody - Jew and Gentile alike.

How about another example? In the Old Testament, God pours out his wrath on his enemies, and Psalmists ask the Lord to beat up their enemies and kill their enemies' children. Should we do the same? Well, in the New Testament, God still moves against his enemies, but are those enemies still foreign nations aligned against Israel? Are they still particular ethnic groups? No, they are religious people who self-righteously believe that they are superior to everyone else. They are people who reject Christ even when they should know better. Satan and evil spiritual forces are God's enemies, as are those who exploit and oppress the poor and the needy, and those who reject God's love, choosing to live to please themselves instead of living to help others. Regimes that persecute and kill innocents are God's enemies. In short, these are the kinds of enemies we want to see overthrown. But Jesus and his disciples don't call on us to take up the sword in order to start the purging. They tell us that God will take care of it in his time. And they tell us not to regard the poor, the sick, the needy in body or spirit, the spiritually ignorant, the people struggling with righteousness, the sinners, the drunkards, the prostitutes, the tax collectors, and those who are of different races and from different backgrounds as our enemies. And they tell us to pray for our enemies so that God might bring them to repentance, too. God's last words about his enemies and ours through Jesus and the apostles take the mercy that is there in the Old Testament, although it is admittedly well hidden at times, and make it very explicit.

Here's one last example. Though the Old Testament is chock full of God's patience, mercy, and grace, there are many passages which could lead one to believe that God is easily irritated and that he is just sitting around waiting to smite anybody and everybody who steps, even a little ways, out of line. Is this the nature of God? If so, how does he feel about us? After all, we're always stepping out of line!

The cross of Jesus Christ answers those questions, doesn't it? God sacrificed his Son so that we would be reconciled to him and be adopted as his sons and daughters. No longer are we objects of his wrath. We need to interpret the Old Testament through the lens of Jesus and the apostles. They help bring our God and his ways into clearer focus.

Tip 6: Don't Sweat The Stuff You Can't Understand

The young Christian on the other end of the phone was agitated. He had just read Genesis 6:1-7 and felt that he HAD to know who the sons of God were and how they were able to marry the daughters of men, and why the Lord was so upset by this, and who exactly the Nephilim were.

I told him that no one really knew for sure the answers to his questions, but I explained to him the different theories Bible scholars and historians put forth, and I let him know which theory I personally found the most satisfying.

But he himself was far from satisfied. He had to know which of the answers was THE RIGHT ONE. He even lamented that his faith itself was in jeopardy if he couldn't solve these ancient riddles, because maybe they showed him that the Bible didn't make sense and couldn't be trusted.

At this point, I got a little bit sarcastic. (Pastors are only human, you know!) I said, "Oh really? Your faith is in jeopardy? Tell me, what possible difference does it make in God's calling on your life to follow Jesus and to love other people the way Jesus loved them today for you to know who the 'sons of God' were back at the dawn of time? Are you going to be suddenly treating other people differently at work and at home today because you don't understand who the Nephilim were?"

I was counseling the young man to do what a pastor had once counseled my high school friends and I to do: Live by what you can understand in the Bible and don't sweat the rest of it. We, like many teenagers, had told him we were trying to discover what God's will was for our lives. Where should we go to college? Who should we marry? What careers should we pursue? The pastor said, "God has clearly spelled out for you what his will for you is in the Bible. Don't gossip. Don't blaspheme. Love God. Don't worry. Watch out for the poor and the weak. Maybe if you'll start doing these things he has already told you, he will get around to revealing the other things later." And the pastor was right.

When it comes to interpreting the Bible, we need to put into practice what God has already clearly told us and trust that he will make other mysterious things clear to us, if he so chooses, in time.

And we need to make sure we are grasping the big picture the Bible is presenting and not getting bogged down in details that can confuse and frustrate us.

For example, readers of the Gospels have noticed that Jesus talks much differently in the Gospel of John than he does in Matthew, Mark, and

Luke. In fact, if you compare Jesus' words in John to John's writings in his epistles and Revelation, you'll discover that Jesus in John's Gospel sounds an awful lot like, well, John. But should this trouble us? Why couldn't John have decided to present Jesus' teachings to us in his own words? We do this sort of thing all of the time. If over a Sunday dinner, Grandpa asks the question, "What did the preacher talk about this morning?" family members will respond, not by directly quoting the preacher, but by putting what the preacher said into their own words. When reading John's Gospel, we need to keep in mind that we are receiving Jesus' teachings through one of the men he himself appointed as one of his interpreters, and not get bogged down in the question of how many of John's quotes were exactly as Jesus originally said them. The "big picture" is that we are receiving a revelation of Jesus Christ. The "details" include which quotes of Jesus were rephrased, or interpreted, or expanded upon, by inspired John. It's the "big picture" that matters. The "details" do not.

I'll give one last example. Modern day readers, with our knowledge of genetics, puzzle over the story in Genesis 30 of how Jacob gained a flock of speckled and streaked animals for himself by making the animals mate in front of striped branches. How is this possible, we ask? But though the original author may have wanted to show how clever the old Jewish Patriarch Jacob was by using a technique that we now know to be discredited, the main point of the Jacob story from start to finish is that he prospers because God is with him and is blessing him after Laban had cheated him. This becomes especially clear when you read Genesis 31. So the main idea of the story is that God was seeing injustices and was correcting them. Does it really matter whether people back then believed striped sticks in front of animals in heat had anything to do with it or not?

When reading the Bible, go for the big

pictures and latch on to what God has unequivocally said to you, and don't sweat the small stuff, the details, and the things you can't understand. God can make things clearer to you as time goes on. And if he doesn't, it really doesn't matter that much. The "big picture" of the Bible - love God with all you are and love your neighbors like you love yourself - is enough to keep us intrigued and busy for a lifetime. Whether or not I ever find out what kind of fish swallowed Jonah or what baptism for the dead means (1 Corinthians 15:29) are pretty much small potatoes in comparison.

Tip 7: Let The Church Guide Your Interpretation Of Scripture

For twenty-one centuries the Holy Spirit has been at work guiding the people of God as they have studied and applied the Bible. And Jesus gave the Apostles the keys to understanding the truths of the kingdom of God (Matthew 16:13-19; John 14:25-26). The early Christians searched the scriptures (Acts 17:10-11) and were given the task of pronouncing judgment over whether or not messages were truly from God (1 Corinthians 14:29; 1 Thessalonians 5:19-22).

So, how likely do you think it is that people today can come up with entirely novel interpretations of God's truths? Not very likely. This is not to say that The Church can't come up with new ways to apply God's unchanging Truth to our ever-changing world, or that Bible scholars can't discover new ways to look at things which are based on the orthodox understandings of the past, or that as more of the historical settings and cultural backgrounds of the Bible's original authors come to light, their words won't become clearer to us, etc. But it is to say that if a person or a group or a denomination or a cult comes up with interpretations and applications that have no basis in church history, or if they claim to teach Truth as it has never been known before, or if they promise to tell you Christianity's "real story" that has been suppressed for ages, then those interpretations and applications are very suspect - to say the least! As one of my seminary profs said sarcastically about a relatively new theology, "So for nineteen centuries The Church and The Holy Spirit had gotten things wrong, and we were all just waiting for this new school of thought to come along and lead us out of the dark ages." And as another prof exhorted us, "As preachers you are supposed to be accurate, interesting, and relevant. But you're not supposed to be original." He wasn't telling us that we shouldn't bring our imaginations to bear on the scriptures and on our illustrations in order to bring God's Word to life for our congregations, but he was warning us that we weren't supposed to come up with novel ideas that nobody in The Church had ever thought of before.

All of this really hit home to me one night when a friend of mine introduced me to his new girlfriend who was supposedly a Christian. She began to talk about her new faith, and red flags started going off in my mind. She described two different types of "holy spirit" that believers can receive. When she spoke about Christ, she kept stressing the MAN Jesus and how he really wasn't much different than we are. She said that he had become a kind of "god," but we can be that kind of a "god," too. And she had a pet name for Satan which made it sound as though temptation and sins weren't really big deals. She had learned all of this from a Bible teacher who was charging money for his lessons, claiming that he had discovered the way the Bible was actually supposed to be taught, but hadn't been since the days of the Apostles. The things she was saying certainly weren't matching up with any sort of historic Christianity I had ever encountered, and when I returned home that night, I began doing some research. Sure enough, it turned out that she had joined a cult and it was one that was scamming impressionable young people out of their money. The Holy Spirit had used what I knew about how God had guided The Church in the past to help me discern that the young woman was being deceived in the present.

Don't be deceived. When Bible interpretations don't match what The Spirit has said to the churches down through the ages, reject them. Maybe you won't run into cultists, but you may run across books that promise to reveal "The Hidden

Secrets Of Numerology in The Bible," or how Ezekiel's flying wheels were really flying saucers. I once met a lady who somehow believed that she needed to "cook" her prayers in some kind of pot before they would be able to reach God. Where in Church history would you ever find things like that?

And it is common nowadays for ancient books like the Gospel of Thomas or the Gospel of Judas to be trotted out before the public as "secret, important, suppressed documents" that The Church doesn't want you to read. The truth is that these books have never been suppressed, and have always been available, but were rejected by The Church, guided by the Holy Spirit, as not containing God's Truth. Not to mention that they have been historically discredited and have been proven to be more about promoting certain philosophies and heresies than they are about accurately giving us pictures of Jesus and his followers.

Trust what The Spirit has said through The

Church, Christ's Body, down through the centuries. Let recognized and accepted Christian Truth guide you in your interpretations of the Bible. Are your interpretations in harmony with the Apostle's Creed, the Nicene Creed, etc.? And find out what your denomination or your church says on subjects relating to understanding the Bible and theology. Many denominations and churches have literature or websites available where their positions are spelled out, and often even give you the history of how those positions were arrived at. Let God's people of the past guide your thoughts in the present.

Tip 8: Give The Biblical Authors The Right To Talk Like Real People Do

If on a Friday night in our high school's gymnasium, I looked around and said, "Boy, everybody in town's at the basketball game tonight," anyone who heard me would know that I was remarking on the size of the crowd. They would know I didn't mean that literally everyone in town was there. The nursing home didn't cart all its residents to the game. People with the flu stayed home. Families in town who had sons and daughters attending other school districts stayed away. But what I said would be accepted as a normal, human way of exaggerated speaking in order to make a point.

Yet critics of the Bible, when they run across

statements like, "The whole town came out to see Jesus," will scoff and ask, "How could that really be possible that a whole town left what it was doing and crowded around Jesus?" The critics won't give the biblical authors the right to use normal, exaggerated human speech to make their points.

Or, when some believers run across David's poems in the Psalms where he goes on and on about how much he loves God's law and meditates on it day and night and how he pants for the law and finds his highest and truest delight in it, they feel guilty because they know that they don't have David's level of devotion and seem unable to work it up within their hearts. But they forget that David is speaking in poetry. He is writing love songs to God. And the language of song and of poetry is not literal. For example, if someone today writes a love song about a girl named Mary and says he thinks about nothing but her eyes day and night, we know he doesn't mean that literally. For one thing, he has to sleep sometime. For another thing, I doubt that when his boss is calling him on the carpet for not getting a report in on time that he's thinking about how Mary's eyes are brown. Instead he's expressing in his song that he loves Mary, and he's urging us to appreciate what is great about her, too. He's idealizing his love for her, making it sound as perfect as he wished it was, but he's not to be taken literally. When biblical poets and song writers express their love for God, urge us to appreciate his greatness and join them in song, and when they idealize their love for him, making it sound as perfect as they wish it was, they are expressing truths and emotions to us and urging us to love God and to grow in our appreciation of him, but they don't want us to flagellate ourselves because we don't literally fulfill every poetic phrase they've written. We need to let biblical poets talk like real poets. (Incidentally, when David was discouraged and needed Jonathan to help him find strength in the Lord, or when he watched Bathsheba bathe on her rooftop and then slept with her and had her husband murdered, or when he ignored the discipline of his children, or when he took a census that the Lord disapproved of, he wasn't exactly meditating on how precious the law of God was at those times, was he?)

Regular human beings use different types of speech and different forms of literature in order to communicate ideas. If I'm telling a joke, I try to keep it short and simple and use puns and wordplays. If I'm writing a press release for an upcoming event at our church, I try to make it enticing and I stick to answering the who, what, where, when, and the "how much it will cost" kinds of questions. If I'm writing a term paper, I marshal my arguments in great detail and try to back up what I'm saying by using references. If I'm writing a business letter, I adopt a much different tone than I do when I'm emailing an old pal from my college days.

The biblical authors were real people and they used figures of speech, metaphors, similes, stories, and even jokes and puns which would have been familiar to their audiences. For instance, in the Bible days, when the world order would change - a government would fall, a new ruler would come to power, a battle would turn out unexpectedly, etc. - writers would use language about the heavens being shaken, the stars falling, the moon turning to blood, the earth splitting apart. Today we might say something like, "The world turned upside-down" to express the same thing. And we wouldn't mean it any more literally than the ancient writers did.

In the Bible, various authors wrote laws, official edicts, poetry, genealogies, parables, stories, historical accounts, philosophical inquiries, prophecies, words of protest and indictment against the rulers of God's people and other nations, letters to church groups and to individuals, dreams and visions, and they wrote apocalypses - writings that talked about current events and future events using code words lest they fall into the wrong hands, and couching everything in terms of events and battles taking place in the heavenly realms and on Earth. And some writers wrote Gospels, which were not exactly biographies. They were books designed to let readers know that good news had come in the person of an extraordinary teacher and ruler. Gospels followed themes and weren't as concerned with "then the leader did this and he followed it up by doing that" as biographical writers would be today. We can think of the Gospels as being sort of like the political biographies that are written every four years to introduce Presidential candidates and to tell us why we need them.

When we are reading, interpreting, and applying the words of the ancient writers today, we need to recognize the types of literature they are using and how they fashion language to get their points across. Then we'll know when they mean for us to take what they are saying literally and when, instead, they are using other communication tools rather than literal speech to convey their God-inspired emotions, ideals, truths, dreams, guidance, and insight to us. The authors were real people and they will communicate as real people to us, if we will let them, instead of concluding that when Jesus says he longs to gather the Jews under his wing that he is a chicken, or that when Paul commands us to pray without ceasing that it would be a sin for you to study a menu in a restaurant and decide what you want for lunch.

Tip 9: Remember That God Is The Hero Of The Bible

The Bible contains many great stories of heroes of the faith. And there's even a famous chapter, Hebrews 11, which lists examples of men and women whose faith in God is commended and rewarded. But in the Bible Hebrews 11 comes after Hebrews 10 - which urges us to hold onto our own faith so that we will be saved - and before Hebrews 12 - which uses the list of heroes in Hebrews 11 to inspire us to persevere in our own races in life and even to faithfully endure God's discipline if a heavenly Father sees fit to send it our way. So, Hebrews 11, with its listing of the giants of biblical faith, is meant to encourage us in our own faith and to exhort us to be giants ourselves.

Too often, though, when we think about the

men and women in the Bible, we can easily become discouraged. After all, Moses raised his staff and parted the Red Sea. Abraham was willing to sacrifice his son, Isaac, to the Lord. David killed Goliath. Esther saved her people from extermination. Peter walked on water. Paul was bitten by a poisonous viper and just shook it off with no ill effects. John was taken up into the throne room of God. And what have I done for God lately? Hmm? When we compare ourselves to the men and women in the Bible, we often come up short. And we can feel like, "What's the use? I'm not a Moses! I don't have the faith of Elijah! I'm no Stephen who could give a stirring defense of his beliefs and a condemnation of his executors before he was stoned! I'm not a Mary or a Martha who believed Jesus could raise their brother from the dead and had his tomb opened! The Bible tells the stories of exceptional people, and I'm not exceptional. I'm average at best, and most of the time I'm hoping God is going to grade on the curve or I'm sunk."

But, actually, the Bible doesn't tell the stories of exceptional people. It tells the story of an exceptional God. And it lets us know the exceptional things he can do with below average people - with sinners - like us.

Harry Wendt, the founder of Crossways International, doesn't like the term, "heroes of the faith," because, as he says, if you actually read the stories in the Bible, you will discover that the so-called "heroes" are all skunks. But that's okay, he says, because he himself is a skunk and so are you. If God could use the skunks in the Bible, then he can use us skunks who are around today.

And, indeed, apart from Jesus Christ, who was the extraordinary God incarnate, the "heroes" of the faith *were* skunks. Abraham, after exhibiting great faith in God's fantastic promise, later had his doubts and he and his wife tried to find a way to fulfill God's plan their own way, not the Lord's. And speaking of his wife, Abraham was willing to give her away to become part of a king's harem in order to save his own skin.

Let's quickly look at some more of the "great heroes" of the Bible and discover their skunk-like characteristics:

- Jacob was a deceiving momma's boy.
- Joseph was the typical bratty favored little brother that all older siblings can't stand.
- Moses tried to escape God's call on his life and later disobeyed the Lord and was forbidden to enter the Promised Land.
- King David committed adultery, then tried to cover it up just as if he was one of the crooked politicians of our day, and finally resorted to murder to get the husband out of the picture.
- Jeremiah was a manic-depressive.
- Jonah was a vengeful, bigoted racist.
- Jesus' disciples fought over which one of them was the greatest.

- John the Baptist, despite all he knew of Jesus, still wasn't sure that Jesus really was the Messiah.
- Mary and Jesus' brothers thought Jesus was crazy and tried to take charge of him and put him away somewhere.
- Peter denied knowing Jesus three times and, later on in his ministry, needed Paul to rebuke him because he was snubbing the Gentile believers in favor of a Jewish group from Jerusalem that he was afraid of.

If we read the Bible with the mindset of "Oh, I wish I could be a Daniel, or a Moses, or a Paul," we are missing the point. We should read the Bible rejoicing that, "I have the same God as Daniel, Moses, and Paul." We need to read the Bible remembering that, "The God of the Bible is the same yesterday, today, tomorrow, and forever. And so, the God who graciously used skunks back then will still graciously use them today. I wonder how he will choose to use me?"

Likewise, if we read the Bible with the mindset, "It was easy to believe in God back then when he was doing miracles and speaking out loud all the time," we miss the point. The Bible covers many centuries, and the times God performed miracles or spoke are rare. And there are books in the Bible - Ruth, Esther, Ecclesiastes, Song of Songs, Philemon - where nothing overtly supernatural seems to happen at all. The point is that the same God who sustained believers in the past who were living their daily lives as we do, without miracles around every corner, will sustain us and keep us faithful, too.

God is the hero of the Bible. He created the universe. He won't let Satan mess it up. He arranges history according to his plans. He continually does the impossible - including providing a way for sinners to be forgiven and to become his sons and daughters. He secretly works out the glorious future in which all will be redeemed. When we read the Bible, we are reading the amazing story of a great hero. And he's not a hero who lived long ago. He's alive now. He's our hero today. His heroic deeds continue. And we are his servants, his soldiers, and his sons and daughters who are being transformed into the image of Christ, so, with God's help, we can perform God's deeds. We're part of God's on-going heroic story.

Tip 10: Realize That The Bible Is A Call To Action

A Black man once was speaking bitterly about the life his mother had led as she tried to raise children by herself in the Projects. She had to hold down multiple jobs in a vain attempt to make ends meet. And he said that she kept right on reading promises in the Bible of a better life that never materialized and kept right on praying prayers for deliverance from the ghetto which never came. As far as he could tell, his mother's faith had been worthless. Now, to be fair, he doesn't know whether his mother's faith gave her the strength to get up another day, or if it affected how she treated her children and others. Her faith may have indeed been a very important element in making her the woman she was.

But the man saw only that the Bible offered her personal bromides and spiritual placebos and pithy little sayings that could be embroidered on tea towels and hung around the apartment. It primarily provided small bandages for hemorrhaging cuts and kept putting the same old dressings on reopened and un-healing wounds.

I have to say that if that man's view of the Bible is correct, that it is primarily a book of feel good-isms or a "Chicken Soup for the Soul," then the Bible does indeed fail miserably. And even worse than that, it gives people false hopes and is an opiate for the masses to keep the people from thinking too much about their true miserable lots in life.

But is that what the Bible really is? When Jesus appeared to his disciples after his resurrection, he didn't instruct them, "Now get together every day and sing praise songs about how great it is to be Christians. And keep looking on the sunny side, always on the sunny side, of life." No, instead he called them to go out into the world and make disciples of all nations. He told them that all authority had been given to him and, yes, he promised to be with them always, to the very end of the age. But his authority and his presence would be manifested to them as they went out into the world to change lives by teaching people to follow Christ. He didn't tell them, "Stick around Jerusalem and I'll promise you that whatever problems you encounter there, I will straighten out for you." He told them to leave and get out into the world! But, instead, the disciples got too comfortable in Jerusalem, so God sent persecution to get them to scatter into the world and make a difference wherever they went. Oh, and Jesus told them that when they went out in the world they would find troubles. As the old song says, "He didn't promise them a rose garden." He promised them a cause worth giving their lives to and for.

From the very start of God's dealings with

humanity, God wanted men and women to be involved with the world he had made. Adam and Eve were given the tasks of subduing the earth, caring for the garden, and naming the animals. When the Lord called Abraham to form a new community of humanity, it was so that through Abraham's line all nations and peoples of the world would eventually be blessed. God's purpose in calling Israel to be his special nation was so that the other nations would want the kind of relationship and blessings Israel had with its God for themselves. Jesus called on his followers to be salt and light to the world. In other words, his followers were to give the world its flavor and to preserve the ethical order of the world by reminding those around them of the ways of God. And his followers were to provide light by doing good deeds and letting those deeds shine forth so that everyone could see them and then praise their Father in heaven (Matthew 5:13-16).

    Christians aren't saved by doing good works.

Only the grace of God operating in Christ saves us. But we are saved in order for us to do good works, the works that God prepared in advance for us to do in order to bring his good news to the world (Ephesians 2:8-10).

Rather than looking at the Bible as primarily a source of personal comfort (though God's Word indeed gives comfort at times), or as a source of verses we can put on posters featuring kittens and wide-eyed cartoony-looking children, we should view the Bible as the Field Manual for God's Army. It tells us how to engage the sin we find in the world and in our own hearts. It tells us how to engage the wrong thinking we find in the world and in ourselves. It explains how we are to live as members of God's Army and as his representatives, his family, in the world. It orders us to engage our real enemies - the world, the flesh, and the devil.

Every great commanding officer cares for his troops. And we have the greatest commanding officer ever, because he is also our heavenly Father. But every great commanding officer also cares about the mission those troops are on. And while he wants to see the physical and psychological needs of his troops met and wants them to stay healthy as long as possible, and wants them to be as well-trained and as well-equipped as necessary in order to fight the enemy, even the greatest commanders know that some troops are going to be lost. They are going to be expendable for the greater good, the mission. And so it is with God's Army, too. The book of Revelation commends believers who were faithful even to the point of death, and urges all Christians to be just as faithful. In the "Faith Chapter," Hebrews 11, believers are commended for refusing to be released when tortured, and they were imprisoned, stoned, sawed in half, and left destitute in the world because they refused to give in to the world (Hebrews 11:35-40).

I once heard a Christian poet say that she

wanted pictures of children and puppies to be on the cover of her next book because, she said, "Jesus lives in children and puppies." I wonder what Jesus she was referring to? Certainly not the one who said he hadn't come to bring peace to the earth, but a sword. Certainly not the one who drove the moneychangers out of the temple using a whip. Certainly not the one who said that violent men take the kingdom of God.

It's time that we stopped approaching the Bible in order to (if you'll allow me to paraphrase John Kennedy) ask what it can do for us, but rather ask what it would have us do for our world. It's our marching orders from King Jesus. Let it motivate us to bring relief to the poor, visit the sick and lonely, speak out against corruption, speak up for life, proclaim freedom for Satan's captives, take stands against racism, banish the clouds of guilt many live under, bring hope that goes beyond this life, and do everything else it sends us into the world to do. The

Bible isn't meant to make us comfortable. It's meant to make us committed.

Tip 11: Feel Free To Skip Some Parts

When my friends and I were training to become pastors, our professors impressed on us the importance of "preaching the whole counsel of God." What they meant was that we should make sure we were using the whole Bible in our preaching and teaching, and that we shouldn't fall into the lazy and easy trap of just relying on our favorite books or on passages that we were very familiar with. And I have known preachers whose sermons each sound about the same. They always give basic "come to Jesus" salvation messages or rail against the evils of alcohol, sex, drugs, and rock-n-roll. Their congregations aren't really getting fed a balanced diet from God's Word. It's like the people are getting cheeseburgers and French fries for every spiritual meal. They end up spiritually malnourished.

But pastors aren't the only ones guilty of sticking to the same old subjects and the same old Bible passages. I have known Christian laypeople who claim familiarity with the Bible, but can really only quote, or even talk about, such well-known chestnuts as Psalm 23, John 3:16, the Beatitudes (Matthew 5), and the Love Chapter (1 Corinthians 13). They have only ever eaten part of the spiritual meal that God has prepared for them, and they consequently find themselves undernourished, unhealthy, and even malformed. Consequently, they are not strong enough to face and overcome the trials of life.

A continuous diet of only certain promises or selected subjects is spiritually unhealthy and makes it difficult to fully grow up in Christ. The promises may be precious when you need them, but you also need the spiritual vitamins a good struggle with the book of Job can provide.

There are times in life when we have to turn to specific passages to deal with our specific needs.

Though I definitely believe all Christians should regularly expose themselves to all of the Word of God (there are plans and books available to help the average person read through the entire Bible in 1-5 years), I also believe that it's okay for Christians to sometimes skip over entirely, or lightly skim through, some parts of the Bible, because at certain times in their lives, those parts wouldn't be helpful.

Since God's Word is his communication to us, there will be times when we will need to converse with him about certain urgent topics, like dealing with sexual sins, for example, but if we open up the book of Exodus and read about the building of the Tabernacle it will just seem to us as though God has gone way off topic.

The Bible is also God's manual for his army.

So if you are trying to discover his orders for dealing with persecution, then reading about two lovers desiring each other in Song of Songs probably isn't going to do you much good.

And the Bible is God's Fatherly words of advice and comfort to us. If you are saddened over the death of a loved one and want to talk to your heavenly Father about it, reading Ezekiel's prophecy against Edom probably isn't going to do much for you.

When giving new believers portions of the Bible to read for the first time, tell them to feel free to skip the parts they find boring, because we've all known of young Christians who were so excited to start reading the Bible only to get all bogged down in the "who begot whos" and give up in frustration. They aren't yet ready for the more human parts of God's incarnate Word - such as the records of who was related to which family groups - and usually need something a little more clearly divine to start with.

The Gospel of Mark is a good place for new converts to start because it tells the story of Jesus in a fast-moving, action-oriented style. The Gospel of John tells the story of Jesus in a more poetic style. Some readers may prefer that.

An army officer wouldn't give a new recruit the specifics to automated weapons before first introducing him or her to the concept of a handgun and how to use and care for it. Sometimes we have introduced new Christian recruits to more advanced ideas and methods of spiritual warfare and wonder why they aren't catching on to what we are saying, when what they really needed was a course on the basics.

To sum up, God provides spiritual vegetables, fruits, salads, herbs, nuts, meat, and wine in his Word. And we need all of it. But sometimes in life, we need some of the comfort food - the spiritual mashed potatoes, meatloaf, and ice cream he also provides. And that's okay, too, and we don't have to feel guilty for craving, and enjoying, it.

Tip 12: Don't Study The Bible As A Purely Intellectual Exercise

A famous author/philosopher once investigated the Bible's claims and came to the conclusion that the Bible was indeed the Word Of God and was true. So, he was asked, "Does this mean that you now want to be a Christian?" His answer was startling. "No," he said. "If I did that, I would have to change my life too much and I like my life the way it is now." The author obviously was missing the point of Bible study. We don't just study the Bible because we find it interesting, or curious, or fascinating, or because it is part of our cultural heritage, or because it contains some great literature, or even just because it is true. We study the Bible in order to encounter God. We read the Bible so that God can communicate with us, motivate us, convict us, and change us to be more like Jesus Christ.

Most Christian churches view the Bible as one of "the means of grace." In other words, it is one of things that God has given us that brings his grace into our lives. This means that something supernatural happens, or is supposed to happen, when we expose ourselves to the Bible. God will be working in our hearts, souls, and minds, bringing us grace.

"Don't Study The Bible As A Purely Intellectual Exercise." This is a dangerous tip for me to include in this book, because for much of this book I have stressed using your mind when you read, study, and apply the Bible. I've talked about such things as learning about the cultural backgrounds of the original authors and readers, remembering that the authors used different types of literature and writing styles, and letting the authors interact with each other. And I don't take back anything that I've written.

But in stressing the intellect, I don't want to give anyone the impression that you study the Bible the same way that you would study a history book or a science book or a book that's a collection of pieces of ancient literature. When we study the Bible we should do it prayerfully and expectantly, waiting for God to speak to us. And we should do it with our hearts and minds wide open, ready for whatever challenges and changes the Lord brings our way as we immerse ourselves in his Word.

Otherwise we are wasting our time. 2 Timothy 3:15-17 says that the scriptures are able to make us wise for salvation, to teach, correct, and train us, so that we can be thoroughly equipped for every good work. If we aren't using the Bible for those purposes, then it's like God has given us a beautiful diamond ring, but we only use it whenever we have some pieces of glass we need to cut. We aren't using it the way the giver intended. And the book of James warns us, "Do not merely listen to the word, and so deceive yourselves. Do what it says. Anyone who listens to the word but does not do what it says is like a man who looks at his face in the mirror and, after looking at himself, goes away and immediately forgets what he looks like" (James 1:22-24). In other words, there is no lasting benefit to him. Verse 25 goes on to say, "But the man who looks intently into the perfect law that gives freedom, and continues to do this, not forgetting what he has heard, but doing it - he will be blessed in what he does."

Because the Bible is communication from a living God, we don't ever have to despair that we will reach a point where we will totally exhaust its wisdom. I have been an ordained pastor since 1982, and I still discover new things in the Bible as I study. As I grow in faith and in life experiences, biblical texts that didn't say much to me when I was younger suddenly jump off the pages at me now. Just as we grow to understand and appreciate our parents as we learn more about them observing them through the years, so we grow to understand and appreciate God as we continue to have an ongoing relationship with him. And have parents or friends ever surprised you by doing something totally unexpected and left you wondering where that came from and if there are aspects of their personalities that you never dreamt of before? So, God in the scriptures and in life will surprise you and set you back on your heels. An infinite God is communicating to our finite minds, so we'll find, as the Bible says, his mercies to be new every morning. I don't mean to imply that every time you pick up the Bible you'll be hit with something exciting, unusual, and different. Relationships don't work that way. Every single day with your spouse or your roommate isn't going to be "like new," but over time, treasures and surprises will still surface.

The story of the famous author/philosopher

had a happy ending. He did finally become a Christian, submitting to God's Word and entering into a relationship with him, instead of just learning about him. And I hope your story of studying, reading, and applying God's Word has a happy ending, too.

Appendix 1: For Further Study

(Disclaimer: I don't agree with everything these authors say or with all of their denominational stances, but I still recommend their books.)

Recommended For Further Study

Crossways International, http://www.crossways.org. Courses and material designed to get the Bible's main message across, or to go into in-depth study of topics and biblical books.

Eerdmans Handbook to the Bible, by David Alexander (author), Pat Alexander (editor), Grand Rapids: Eerdmans, 1992. General information about every book in the Bible and biblical times.

Knowing Scripture, by R.C. Sproul, Downer's Grove: InterVarsity Press, 2009. Great introduction to reading the Bible.

New Bible Commentary: 21st Century Edition, by Carson, France, Motyer (authors), Wenham (editor), Downer's Grove: InterVarsity Press, 1994. Commentaries for laypersons on every book in the Bible collected in one volume.

Recommended For A Little More Serious Study

How To Read The Bible For All Its Worth, 3rd Edition, by Gordon D. Fee, Douglas Stuart, Grand Rapids: Zondervan, 2003. Talks about different translations and commentaries and the merits of each and explains how to read and interpret the different types of literature and books found in the Bible.

The IVP Bible Background Commentary: Old Testament by Walton, Matthews, Chavalas (authors), Downer's Grove: InterVarsity Press, 2000. Doesn't focus on spiritual and inspired aspects of scripture, but on the cultures the Old Testament literature came from.

The IVP Bible Background Commentary: New Testament, by Craig S. Keener, Downer's Grove: InterVarsity Press, 1994. Doesn't focus on spiritual and inspired aspects of scripture, but on the cultures the New Testament literature came from.

Recommended For Very Serious Studies

Abusing Scripture: The Consequences Of Misreading The Bible, by Manfred T. Brauch, Downer's Grove: InterVarsity Press, 2009. Explores the ways we misunderstand and misuse the Bible and how this damages The Church, individual believers, and our witness to the world. Also gives many keys to properly interpreting scripture.

Slaves, Women & Homosexuals: Exploring The

Hermeneutics Of Cultural Analysis, by William J. Webb, Downer's Grove: InterVarsity Press, 2001. Gives principles of how to determine what things in the Bible are eternal truths and which were relevant to the cultures of their times using the examples of what the Bible says about slavery, women, and homosexuals. Also encourages us to find the direction the Holy Spirit is moving and to get in step with Him.

Appendix 2: Six Common Mistakes People Make When Approaching Bible Study

Mistake 1. Taking the words of a pastor, Bible teacher, author, the notes in your Study Bible, or a commentary as being THE Word of God, instead of realizing that they are the opinions (hopefully informed opinions) of human beings.

Mistake 2. Believing that a particular version of the Bible is THE Word of God, rather than recognizing it as the work of paraphrasers or translators who (hopefully) tried to convey the meaning of the original ancient languages the Bible was written in.

Mistake 3. Seeking some great spiritual motivation or mystical insights before you begin to read the Bible, feeling somehow that you aren't worthy to delve into the scriptures, instead of remembering that the Bible was written for common people and that you begin to read it as you would any book - pick it up and just start!

Mistake 4. Feeling that insights you gain or questions you have aren't worth sharing with other Christians, forgetting that you are a member of The Church - The Body of Christ - and that the Lord gave you to your brothers and sisters, and they to you, for a reason.

Mistake 5. Getting puffed up when you do get insights from God's Word, instead of remaining teachable all of your life and remembering that God's Wisdom is offered to the simple (Proverbs 9:1-12).

Mistake 6. Using the "monkey see, monkey do" method of interpreting scripture, instead of remembering that people in the Bible did bad things we shouldn't imitate, and that the Bible records what God and believers did in situations in the past and these stories don't necessarily tell us what God will always do and what believers should always do.

Appendix 3: An Exercise in Misapplying the Bible

For me, part of the process of reading and digesting a book is talking back to its author in my mind. And lately a question I've been asking lots of authors is, "Haven't you ever read the rest of the Bible?" It seems to be that more and more authors today pull a bunch of verses relating to their topics out of the Bible, expound on them a little, throw in some personal stories and then call their work finished. But sometimes they fail to take into account what the Bible as a whole says about their subjects and have conveniently, whether consciously or unconsciously, ignored scripture passages which may provide a bit of balance to what they are saying, or may even contradict or call into question their basic premises.

It can be dangerous to pull verses out of the Bible, especially if the contexts are ignored, and build beliefs and practices on them. This is called "proof-texting." A person comes up with a slightly, or even more than slightly off-kilter idea and then attempts to prove it by reciting a bunch of selected verses.

Let me show you how ridiculous this approach to theology and biblical interpretation can be by using an important subject, marriage, as an example.

What does the Bible say about marriage? Let's look at some verses. In Genesis 2:18-25, marriage is seen as a God-given solution to loneliness. It brings a sense of completeness to a person and unites a couple in physical and spiritual ways. In the book of Deuteronomy, marriage is seen more as a business deal (Deuteronomy 22:28-29). In ancient Israel, a man would pay the father of a girl a dowry price in order to marry her and it was assumed that the woman would be a virgin. This was important because a man had to make sure that any children that resulted from the marriage, especially the firstborn son, were really his own because of the inheritance laws and the importance of carrying on the family name and of keeping the family's land. So, if a man raped an engaged woman, he would have to pay her father a price for her and marry her. She couldn't marry anyone else because now she wasn't in "brand new, showroom condition" any longer. In Malachi, marriage is a covenant, and God's purpose in establishing it was that believers would produce godly offspring (Malachi 2:13-15). In the Song of Songs, marriage is all about the enjoyment of sex and romantic love aside from procreating. Ephesians 5:22-33 and Revelation 19:6-9 and 21:1-2 tell us that earthly marriage is a picture of the love and union Christ has with The Church. But Paul, in I Corinthians 7, sees marriage as a sort of a necessary evil for some people who can't live on the higher path of sanctified singleness.

What do you suppose would happen to me as a pastor if I were to give a message during a wedding ceremony based solely on I Corinthians 7? "Stan and Sue, you are standing before this congregation today because you can't control yourselves or your passions. How we wish you could! Then you could focus entirely on God and his work and be fulfilled. Oh, what you could accomplish for him! But, it's not to be. So, let's get you married so that you can have sex and Satan won't keep disrupting your prayer life. Marriage will be a good thing for you two. It just won't be the best thing. Thank God that he made a concession to your weakness and will let you become man and wife. Otherwise you would someday roast in Hell."

Or if I gave a message based only on verses from Deuteronomy 22? "Stan, I hope you paid her father a good and fair price for Sue. And remember, if you are dissatisfied with her because it turns out she isn't a virgin, then return her to her father and we, the congregation, will stone her."

Or how about a sermonette based on Song of Songs? "Stan and Sue, we know the longing you have to be alone and praise each other's body parts and caress them and kiss them and taste them. It's a longing that is almost driving you mad and making you faint. So we'll cut the wedding and reception short and let you get right to your honeymoon bed before you die of sexual hunger and frustration."

Or one from Malachi? "Go forth from here and begin making babies as soon as you can and make as many as you can because this is a form of church growth that God approves of. And based on what the Old Testament says, let's hope and pray that they are males. Otherwise, Stan, if you die without producing a male heir, one of your brothers will have to sleep with Sue."

I don't think I'd get many "Amens!" from the congregation. In fact, I would probably be fired. And rightly so because I would be giving distorted pictures of marriage which are not based on all the Bible really has to say about the subject. Not to mention that I would be ignoring the circumstances of the people of God and conditions of the world in which they lived that the passages address, and the fact that different literary genres are interpreted differently. For example, Song of Songs is a book of poetry. Exaggeration is one characteristic of poetry. So, no, you won't really collapse unless you see your lover RIGHT NOW! And in I Corinthians 7, Paul believed that some kind of crisis was right around the bend for the church and the world. Maybe he thought that persecution was about to be stepped up or that the Second Coming was about to occur. So, of course, it made sense for him to advocate remaining single and going all out for the Lord.

Yet I continually run across books and articles and speakers which rely on emphasizing certain verses or passages of the Bible while ignoring the rest of it and/or taking words and ideas out of their cultural, historical, and literary contexts in order to expound positions on such diverse subjects as the end times, women's ordination, the daily Christian life, spiritual gifts, human sexuality, and the nature of salvation. But I can't fire any of these authors and some of them are quite famous and their works are best sellers.

I long for the day when the Christian Church wants to examine the Bible in depth, understanding what it's addressing and how it addresses it. And I long for the day in which we become people of The Book, the whole Book, and not just of our favorite passages from it.

Appendix 4: Thirteen-Week Study Guide

This 13-week study guide was prepared for small groups or Sunday School classes to use as they consider together the ideas presented in this book.

Week One

God Said It, I Believed It, And Now I'm All Mixed Up!

1. Mark each of these with either an "**E**" meaning it is an eternal truth, or a "**C**" meaning that it was relevant only for an ancient culture, or a "**?**" if you aren't sure. Discuss your answers.

_____ All the brothers here send you greetings. Greet one another with a holy kiss (1 Corinthians 16:20)

_____ If someone is found doing evil in the eye of the Lord and violating the ways of the Covenant, that person is to be stoned to death (Deuteronomy 17:1-7).

_____ God is our refuge and our strength, an ever-present help in trouble (Psalm 46:1).

_____ Celebrate the Feast of Unleavened Bread. For seven days eat bread made without yeast (Exodus 34:18).

_____ Each one of you should not only look to your own interests, but also to the interests of others (Philippians 2:4).

_____ Now if there is no resurrection, what will those do who are baptized for the dead? If the dead are not raised at all, why are people baptized for them (1Corinthians 15:29)?

_____ Women should keep quiet in the churches and not be allowed to speak. If they have questions they should ask their husbands at home (1 Corinthians 14:34).

2. Mark each of these with either an "**L**" meaning it is to be taken literally, or an "**S**" meaning it is symbolic, or a "**?**" if you don't know. Discuss your answers.

_____ If your eye causes you to sin, gouge it out. If your arm causes you to sin, cut it off (Matthew 5:29-30).

_____ "And surely I am with you always, to the very end of the age" (Matthew 28:20).

_____ If anyone is sick, he should call the Elders of the church. They will pray and the person will be healed. Confess your sins to one another so that you will be healed (James 5:13-16).

_____ "Then I heard the number of those who were sealed: 144,000 from all the tribes of Israel" (Revelation 7:4).

_____ If you worship the Lord your God, your food and water will be blessed. You won't be sick. There will be no miscarriages and you'll live to ripe old ages (Exodus 23:25 &26).

3. Why is the Bible hard to interpret? Why are there so many different denominations and churches with different opinions on what the Bible teaches?

4. Steve Bierly lists some of the dangers of misinterpreting the Bible. Can you think of some more?

Week Two

Remember What The Bible Actually Is

1. Discover and discuss some ways in which the Biblical writers got their materials:

- Luke 1:1-4

- Proverbs 31:1

- Ecclesiastes 1:12-18

- Daniel 10:12; 12:4

- Revelation 1:1-2

2. What weaknesses, questions, or challenges are inherent in God choosing to give us his Word using humans? Why do you think he chose to give us the Bible in this way?

3. "God's Word is both divine and human." What does that statement mean? How is God's Word like Jesus Christ?

4. The authors sometimes didn't understand what they were being inspired to write; sometimes they questioned God; sometimes they even seemed to be wrong. Should this trouble us? 1 Peter 1:10-12; Habakkuk; Acts 1:6-8; 2 Peter 3:15-16; 1 Corinthians 7:29-31 (the New Testament writers seemed to think Christ's Second Coming was right around the corner).

5. How are the writings in the Bible different than sermons or Christian books written today?

Week Three

Realize That The Bible Is Not *Primarily* God's Personal Message To You

1. How does God speak personally to you as you read the Bible?

2. God's Word was addressed to people centuries ago (Isaiah 1:1; Micah 1:1; Luke 1:3-4; Romans 1:7; Galatians 1:1-9; Philemon 1:1-2; 1 Timothy 1:2).

Why and how is it still relevant to you today?

3. Does God give a person a special verse that the person needs for a specific day?

4. How are verses in the Bible different than fortune cookies or daily doses of wisdom from self-help gurus?

5. Are there aspects of, and lessons in, the Bible which don't apply to Christians living in today's world?

Week Four

Let The Authors Of The Bible Debate, Clarify, Enlighten, Contradict, And Correct One Another

1. Should contradictions in the Bible trouble us and cause us to question our faith?

2. Should authors debating with one another in the Bible trouble us and cause us to question our faith?

3. Which of the examples in this book of biblical authors contradicting, or debating with, or correcting each other, or of authors giving more insight than some previous authors grabbed your attention the most?

Can you think of other examples?

4. How do a variety of voices help us find The Truth in the world today?

How do they help us find The Truth in the Bible?

Week Five

Follow The Progression Of Themes And Ideas Within The Bible

1. Think about how the idea of forgiveness of sins progresses through the Bible. How is this idea handled in:

   The Mosaic Law –

   The Prophets –

   The New Testament -

2. Why didn't God tell us everything he wanted us to know about every subject all at once?

3. Discuss how the theme of slavery progresses through the Bible.

4. Are there other themes and ideas that progress through the Bible?

5. How does knowing that ideas and themes progress through the Bible guide our interpretation of the Bible?

Week Six

Recognize Jesus As God's Ultimate Revelation To Humankind

1. If we have questions about God, how will looking at Jesus help answer them?

2. We have more than the words of Jesus in the New Testament. We have the words and the writings of the Apostles and their followers. Why should we give what they say any weight?

3. If Jesus is God's ultimate revelation to humanity, why do we need the Old Testament?

4. Why did Jesus have the right to change some of the ideas the Jews followed from the Old Testament? Isn't the Old Testament the Word Of God?

Week Seven

Don't Sweat The Stuff You Can't Understand

1. John Calvin never wrote a commentary on the book of Revelation because he said he couldn't understand it. Should this fact have disqualified him from writing theological books and commentaries on other parts of the Bible?

2. Are there parts of the Bible you don't understand or doctrines the Bible teaches that you can't comprehend? Do these things trouble you or make you doubt your faith? How do you handle the parts you don't understand?

3. How can keeping "the big picture" of the Bible in mind help you as you encounter portions of the Bible which are difficult to believe or understand?

4. Deuteronomy 29:29. This verse can be a guiding philosophy of life and faith. How so?

5. How would you answer a young person's question, "What is God's will for my life?"

Week Eight

Let The Church Guide Your Interpretation Of Scripture

1. In your opinion, where do cults and strange, offshoot Christian groups come from? Why do they attract followers?

2. If you had a question about a biblical passage or a Christian doctrine, where would you go to find answers?

3. The early Church and the Apostles were given the task of understanding and interpreting the truths of the Kingdom of God. Does the modern Church still have this task?

4. How can we determine what The Church teaches about Christian doctrines and biblical passages when there are so many different denominations and Christian groups in the world?

5. How does the concept of The Church as The Body of Christ aid us in our interpretation of scripture?

Week Nine

Give The Biblical Authors The Right To Talk Like Real People Do

1. How do we exaggerate or use figures of speech in our daily conversations? Can you think of examples?

2. The Bible is not just one book, but many books collected in one volume. What are some of the different types of writings, books, literature, and documents that we find in the Bible?

3. How do you interpret poetry differently than prose? Should these principles of interpretation cause us to interpret the Psalms, Proverbs, and Ecclesiastes differently than we do the rest of the Bible?

4. When Paul tells us to "pray without ceasing," do you think he means for us to take him literally? What exactly does he mean?

5. Are there any examples of fiction in the Bible that you can think of?

6. Why is some prophecy so hard to understand?

Week Ten

Remember That <u>God</u> Is The Hero Of The Bible

1. Do heroes in the Bible inspire you, give you hope, discourage you, or frustrate you?

Do you aspire to be like them, or despair of ever being able to make it to their level?

2. Is the Bible a book primarily about God, about humans, or about both?

3. Was it easier to believe in God during biblical times than it is now?

4. How do you respond to this statement: "God is the real, and only, hero of the Bible."

Week Eleven

Realize That The Bible Is A Call To Action

1. How is the Bible different than a book full of inspirational stories and comforting sayings?

2. How would you answer someone who says, "My mother depended upon the promises of the Bible, but her life never changed?"

3. Why does God save us from our sins?

4. Does the Bible exist primarily to comfort us or to make us committed? If it exists to make us committed, to what exactly are we supposed to be committed?

5. Which of these descriptive phrases do you believe applies to the Bible and why:

- A manifesto

- A devotional book

- Religious literature

- God's biography

- A divine view of the world

- A field manual for members of God's army

- A call from God to the World

- A book of ethics

Week Twelve

Feel Free To Skip Some Parts

1. What parts of the Bible do you find the most boring?

Why are they in the Bible?

2. Are there parts of the Bible that you have never read?

Should you feel guilty about this?

3. If you need to have God's Word speak to you about a certain subject, what resources could you use to find those biblical passages?

4. Should every Christian read through the Bible at least once?

5. How can you motivate yourself to read the parts of the Bible that aren't your favorites?

Week Thirteen

Don't Study The Bible As A Purely Intellectual Exercise

1. Should you expect anything to happen to you personally as you study the Bible?

2. Christians call the Bible one of "the means of grace."

What does this mean?

What are the other "means of grace?"

3. How important is it to pray while studying the Bible?

4. Is studying the Bible an intellectual exercise, a spiritual exercise, or both, and why?

5. Is it possible to waste your time studying the Bible? How?

6. Can you ever exhaust all the meaning, insight, and revelation of the Bible?

Can you give examples of how parts of the Bible have spoken to you in deeper ways over the years?

One Last Note From The Author

I hope and pray that this book has been helpful to you in fighting the good fight. Maybe you'd like to post a review on Amazon?

And, if you believe this book is worth sharing, would you please let your friends know about it? But whether you do or don't, may God bless you as you follow him!

Steve R. Bierly

Printed in Great Britain
by Amazon